Kundalini and the Power of the Chakras

Techniques for Awakening Your Third Eye Opening the third eye with a candle.

How to Awaken a Dormant Kundalini

Meditation Academy

TABLE OF CONTENTS

Chapter 1 The Third Eye: What Is the Third Eye?

The third eye (sixth chakra) is located at the bottom of the forehead, centered above the bridge of the nose, between the eyebrows. It is oriented horizontally from front to back. The third eye is your

source of extrasensory perception, the seat of psychic sight and wisdom. Spiritual intuition enters your system in this way, giving you a "global vision" of life, with all its levels of energy interaction. Here resides your clairvoyance, your intuition, and your personal awakening, your gateway to inner and higher knowledge. This chakra works in a unique way with all the others because it has a connection to the root chakra, sacred chakra, solar plexus, throat, and crown.

The third eye governs the eyes, ears, sinuses, nose, pituitary gland, and hypothalamus. When this sixth chakra works well, you communicate adequately with both the inner self and the higher self; from then on, you can accomplish more in terms of inner healing and spiritual growth. This chakra allows you to clearly see your energy problems and lessons, so you can take responsibility. Most therapist practitioners have a very strong, very sensitive third eye because they rely on it to establish their diagnosis in their holistic work. As for the harmonization of your physical body, the more you "exercise" your psychic senses, the more they are refined!

People whose third eye is clogged feel cut off from their intuition and deny the existence of higher levels. Some believe in nothing but what they have learned or experienced in the physical world. Their ability to cope with the ups and downs of life is severely diminished so that they often repeat the same lessons without understanding why or how they should exceed them. The fear here is that of the connection to the inner self and the obligation to face "spiritual" duties. This creates a ball of guilt, blame, and shame that prevents them from taking responsibility for what they have created. The intellectual and creative incapacity, thus envied can settle in these people, who do not progress while others advance. So, it is essential to purify the sixth chakra; otherwise, you will continue to obstruct you!

Emotional problems related to this part of the body are anxiety, paranoia, and psychotic behavior, including schizophrenia, depression, mental and emotional instability. Physical imbalances occur in the area of the eyes, ears, sinuses, nose: they also affect the functionally the pituitary and hypothalamus. The pituitary regulates the endocrine system (the glands that secrete hormones directly into the bloodstream) and, as a result, several bodily processes. The hypothalamus regulates the pituitary, body temperature, as well as your dietary and sexual needs, and your need for sleep. Migraines are lodged there; physically, they come from the organs located in this region or are due to hormonal problems that disequilibrate the other chakras. Conceptual or functional learning disabilities are also governed by the third eye, although they often originate from the crown, which regulates the brain and functions of the central nervous system.

Meaning: Knowing or order Location: Middle forehead Color: Indigo

Element: None

Symbol: Lotus 96 petals

Fundamental principle: Perception and conscious knowledge of the Essence

Function: Intuition

Sensory function: All the senses, also in the form of perception extrasensory.

Endocrine Gland: The pituitary gland has a secretory activity exerting a stimulating function on all other glands. By these stimulants, it harmonizes the glands.

Minerals: Lapis lazuli, indigo sapphire, azurite, Labradorite, silver, quartz crystal

Consciousness:

This chakra is located in the middle of the forehead just above the eyebrows. It is from him that intuition is transmitted to the lower chakras and the mind. This is why Ajna is called the third eye, the eye of intuition.

The third eye is the seat of all awareness processes. We can create new realities on the physical plane like dissolving old realities. In general, this process is automatic and occurs without our conscious intervention. Most of the thoughts that determine our existence are directed by our emotional archetypes blocked or programmed by our own judgments and prejudices, as well as those of others. Thus, the mind is not always the master, but rather the servant of our emotionally charged thoughts that we only partially dominate.

However, these thoughts are realized, literally in our life because what we perceive and live is a manifestation of our subjective reality.

Thanks to the evolution of our consciousness and the gradual opening of the third eye, we are ready to lead this process more and more. Essential knowledge comes to us in the form of intuition, clairvoyance, or any other extra-sensory perception. Thus, everything that we had can only be felt very vaguely becomes a clear and precise perception.

The sixth chakra is the link between our higher consciousness and the ego and between the higher cerebral faculties and the instinctive brain functions.

Linked to the mind, this chakra is represented with two petals that are connected to the right and left lobes of the pituitary and are also attached to the left and right hemispheres of the brain. The right hemisphere is the seat of the intuition; the left is the seat of intelligence. Here takes place the heavenly marriage of the sun and the moon, culminating in the opening of the third eye and the evolved sixth sense. The three main nadis, Ida, Pingala, and Sushumna, unite here before climbing to the crown chakra.

Note the importance of gradually opening this chakra. The complete mastery and balance of the lower chakras is an absolutely necessary condition. Without conscious control of the lower chakras when opening the Ajna chakra, various types of disorientation appear.

1) Harmonious functioning:

Bright spirit, faculty of mental abstraction, good visualization ability, intuitive understanding of many things, open to mystical truths, thoughts animated by idealism and imagination. The detachment of material possessions, fear of death disappears, the gift of telepathy, clear hearing, clairvoyance, access to past lives, and other dimensions.

2) Disharmonious functioning:

"Big head," proud, religiously dogmatic, manipulative and egotistical. Refusal of spiritual knowledge because not scientific and unreal. Try to influence others by the force of thought, to demonstrate power, or to satisfy personal needs.

3) Malfunction:

Dominated by material desires, physical needs, and unthinking emotions. Hypersensitive to the feelings of others, uninsured and unable to distinguish the ego from the higher self. In an extreme case, thoughts can be fuzzy and confused and totally dominated by repressed emotional structures.

Possible causes leading to dysfunction:

1) Physical level:

All that touches the brain, also we find everything that alters consciousness, drugs, alcohol, psychotropic, soothing medications, etc. Sounds too strong or too long, flashes (momentarily), too repetitive words (skull stuffing, indoctrination, hypnotism)

2) Psychoemotional:

Give others the right to think about his place (or let do), to base oneself in his reflection on principles without having understood them, to be delighted in the appearing or the illusions (the style, the conventions) without being aware of it, or preferring to pretend not to see them so as not to spoil their pleasure (for example), not wanting to see the negative of oneself (or that one expresses, etc.) to get over this and make yourself believe that you are "good" and that everything is fine, etc.

3) Spiritually:

Do not succeed in thinking for yourself: by religion or indoctrination, or by giving the authority of your choice to someone else blindly (the spouse, the family, the parents one or more friends, models references to which we do not appropriate the truth).

However, do not forget that it is named here direct influences, there are many indirect influences that may have led to dysfunction, sometimes in relation to the energy of other chakras or the physical, however, one will find the above-named interactions in interrelation.

How to Activate the Third Eye

How to open the third eye is of interest to people who dream of becoming psychics and perceive the world not only as usual with the basic sensory organs. Esotericists are convinced that everyone has inactive abilities. There are special exercises to develop superpowers.

Work with ajna chakra is available to everyone. Initially, the organ of the sixth sense is closed. There are ways to help activate the ajna chakra or third eye. They are used by yogis, esoterics almost regardless of the direction of practice, even among Tibetan monks (according to legends).

While there is a belief that working with an invisible organ threatens with treatment in a mental hospital, it should be noted that the development of abilities does not affect the psyche. The practitioner will gradually gain new opportunities. With the help of the ajna chakra, the world is perceived in a special, supernatural way.

Exercises will be the first steps towards a clairvoyant career. If you set the task of how to open the third eye quickly, you have to first forget about your previous knowledge of the extrasensory.

Working with ajna chakra is not a momentary matter. However, learning to open an additional sense organ is no easier than learning a foreign language. Another important point is the belief in success. Even if the results are not immediately noticeable, without faith in one's own strength, nothing will come of it. Abilities are easily blocked by distrust and thoughts about the impossibility of development.

Techniques for Awakening Your Third Eye Opening the third eye with a candle

This exercise will take a candle. The method is used in the evening or at night, there is no mysticism, but darkness is required. It is advisable to turn off electrical appliances, especially those equipped with LEDs, which distract from the exercise with a candle.

Take a comfortable position, put a candle in front of you, and light it. You need to peer into the flame, focusing only on the fire. They try to blink as rarely as possible, without being too distracted, looking at all the colors in the flame. After a few minutes, unusual shades of fire appear - violet or green. After it was possible to consider all the colors of the flame, close the eyelids. The flame is imprinted on the retina, and it is visible. So you can understand how to open the third eye on your own without paid courses, in the usual home environment.

The blue ball method

This exercise to open the third eye is a form of meditation. Sit comfortably or lie down, achieve inner silence. You can turn on the appropriate mantras or chants that distract from extraneous thoughts and tune in the right way. Relax, breathe evenly, and calmly - your eyes should be closed.

Direct your inner gaze to the area between the eyebrows, where the ajna chakra is located. When you are ready, imagine a blue ball that rotates. The speed and direction of rotation are chosen intuitively, uneven indicators are allowed at different sessions of the task.

As you inhale, imagine how a blue ball draws pure blue energy from the environment into itself. The stream shines and does not raise doubts about the positive direction. There is no need to be afraid that in this way you can "pick up" the negative - problems are possible if the stream turned out to be dirty in appearance, dark and unpleasant.

As you exhale, imagine how the sparkling energy received from the outside world is absorbed by a ball, remains there, condensing the ball. Tension, pressure, and some pain in the area of the eyebrows are a normal reaction to exercises to open the third eye. The optimal time for doing meditation is about 10-15 minutes.

Exercises to open the third eye are necessary for people who want to gain spiritual integrity. There is no need to refuse what nature has granted to man because every person has abilities; just the majority prefers not to work with the Ajna Chakra due to a lack of confidence in mysticism. The development of abilities provides many opportunities that gradually, a person will learn to use.

Breathing technique to help in third eye activation

As noted, the third eye is your ability to see and understand the world beyond the lens of thought. A good way to increase your knowledge of the world and your self-knowledge is to observe your body and your breathing. This is not about studying anatomy in a book, but about focusing on your physical sensations. For this, you can practice physical relaxation, meditation, or sophrology, for example.

Here is a small breathing technique that teaches observation of the body:

- Release your body from top to bottom, from head to toe. Step by step, focus on the sensations of your body as it relaxes: Relax the muscles of the face, neck, shoulders and arms, chest, belly, glutes, and legs.

- Then adopt ventral breathing. When you inhale, the belly swells and welcomes the air. When you exhale, the belly deflates and accompanies the air towards the exit of a soft natural contraction. Breathe in this way over three to four breaths.

- Then take a moment to focus on your body sensations in calm and silence. Observe everything you feel in your body from head to toe.

- Stretch and open your eyes. The exercise is over.

How to Illuminate the Power of the Third Eye Chakra

By repeating this exercise, you will gain a broader awareness of your body, and your mind will learn to plunge into calm and silence.

Meditation - the way to keep your third eye active

Meditation on opening the third eye can be accompanied by pleasant meditative music or mantras. For example, the mantra of intuition, which is associated with the development of dormant opportunities, will do well. The right musical accompaniment for meditation will help you tune in the right mood.

Meditation should be comfortable. Take a comfortable position while lying or sitting. They try several options: sitting in Turkish pose, lying on your back, sitting on a chair in the usual pose. There is one condition - you should relax in the position chosen for meditation, but the back should remain straight.

Stop the internal dialogue. Try not to think about anything; do not talk mentally. Get complete inner silence and maximum concentration on the body or breath. Sometimes, refer to the ajna point. Try to feel pressure, vibration, or heat: sensations mean that everything is done correctly.

Regular meditation is a failsafe way to keep the third eye open.

The dangers of opening the third eye

Your third eye is not inactivated by default for no reason. We are not designed to see what cannot physically be seen. When you activate your third eye, you open your second vision. It means that you begin to perceive and feel the spiritual world. Do not think that from the moment you have activated your third eye, you will spend your days and evenings to see the angels, and you will be in a state of permanent ecstasy.

The spirits that will appear to your vision will be spirits of the astral bottom. The reason being that these are the spirits closest to our physical plane. The worry is that these lost souls will notice that you notice them and will, therefore, begin to come to you. They will appear at any time, no matter if you are driving (I let you imagine the danger), a job interview, in the street, at home, and so on.

These spirits of the lower astral are called "shadow people" within the Anglo-Saxon spiritual community. The "people of the shadows" because they often appear scary, dark, often as shadows.

I live in a house in the countryside. I can tell you that meeting in the middle of the night, walking in my hallway or going back to my room to sleep would be surprising, to say the least.

How to Deal With the Dangers of Opening the Third Eye

These low spirits are to be seen as insects attracted by the light when, in summer, you leave the window open. The activation of your third eye increases your spiritual light, and in doing so, it attracts these spirits as are the mosquitoes by a lamp.

You will be more inclined to perceive and interact with these low spirits that you will not have a spirituality high enough to preserve you. Most people who activate their third eye have only limited spiritual meaning if nonexistent. As a result, they attract to them beings that vibrate to their own vibrations.

It is also very likely that if you have not done work on you, your thoughts, your fears, you will see them appear in demonstrations. The world of the astral is the world of thought, everything that you think is manifested there. If you are a person filled with hatred and anxiety, you will be in contact with the latter, who has taken the form of these "shadow people." Finding yourself face to face with yourself and your own demons is an experience that can be a nightmare.

Many people worry about the dangers of opening the third eye. Well, perhaps not worth it. Just remember that each journey has its own problems and dangers. In every journey you make, problems and dangers will befall you. These dangers will make you stronger as you learn a lot from them. The dangers will make your trip even more interesting. Just be informed about the dangers that may arise and try to overcome them with all your strength and courage!

So, open the third eye or not?

The activation of the third eye should not be an end to itself, and energy work on its lower chakras is indispensable. This allows the circulation of energy in a fluid and safe way. Otherwise, there is a risk of energy imbalance that can not only create significant emotional and spiritual effects, but also physical effects.

A knowledge also of how to manage the activation of the third eye is essential in order to be able to put it in "on/off" mode at will and not to be haunted by day and night visions. Additionally, a knowledge of the spiritual world and its spirits, how to protect yourself and banish them is also essential.

Do not be fooled by the sweet song of the sirens that promise you wonders with the activation of the third eye and be aware of the shadow that also implies. Everyone speaks to you only on the good side but is careful not to warn you about the bad ones. The main reason is that most of these gurus themselves have not activated their third eye and do not know what they are talking about.

I am lucky to have people around me who have activated their third eye, so I have benefited from their experience and direct testimony.

Pay attention. As with everything about the Occult and the Spiritual World, it's not for mere entertainment. We are talking about forces about which most people have no knowledge or experience. Opening such a door can be catastrophic. Opening the third eye is not a hobby or a fad. It must be the result of an important spiritual and magical preparation, be done in a careful and knowledgeable way.

Chapter 2 The Pineal Gland: What Is the Pineal Gland and What Are Its Functions?

It is called pineal because it has the shape of a pineapple and is responsible for the production of serotonin, a substance that regulates our circadian rhythm and controls the life cycles of the human body.

The pineal gland controls the action of light in our body and is located below the cerebral cortex, where two hemispheres of the brain meet. This is the place where the brain regulates consciousness and interprets the sensory and motor functions of the body. Knowing how to activate the pineal gland, people are more open to feelings of ecstasy and unity. They may also have a feeling of understanding everything or a sudden understanding. In addition, when activated, people more easily develop the ability to travel to other dimensions, known as astral projection or side observation.

According to Theosophy, the pineal gland is a source of clairvoyance and intuition, as well as a kind of portal for higher dimensions, since the "third eye" gives us perception beyond the limits of general vision.

How to Activate the Pineal Gland

Activation can be achieved through yoga, meditation, and other more esoteric methods. Here is an exercise that you can perform without leaving your home.

- Sit comfortably and place the index finger of your right hand between the eyebrows, marking the point.

- Concentrate on feeling a finger touch your forehead. Try to feel the heat and throb at this point on your forehead.

- When you clearly feel the pulsation at this point on your forehead, remove your finger and begin to deepen this feeling in your head.

- Then begin to visualize the bright light coming from the top of the head directly to the pulsating point in the center of the eyebrows and inside the head.

- Concentrate on the sensation of pressure at the point on the forehead where light accumulates and enters. You may feel tinnitus and slight discomfort in the forehead, such as pressure.

With this exercise, you activate the third eye and begin to decalcify the pineal gland. This exercise should be repeated daily or several times a day, as you wish. Little by little, you can develop your clarity in dreams, intuition, and clairvoyance.

Why Is the Pineal Gland Blocked?

Researchers claim that the main element that is responsible for calcification of the pineal gland is fluoride in water. Also, chlorine, a low-nutrient diet, processed foods, electromagnetic fields (such as mobile phones), and environmental toxins are harmful to the pineal gland, which is ultimately calcined with substances consisting of calcium phosphate, calcium carbonate, phosphate magnesium, and ammonium phosphate.

Activities and exercises to decalcify the pineal gland

First of all, for this to work, it is imperative to avoid calcium supplements. Artificial calcium supplements are the main cause of calcification. Now, industrial food usually contains calcium in one form or another: calcium phosphate, calcium carbonate, or dicalcium phosphate. So do not eat "all done" anymore, and make smoothies! You will see why.

Raw cacao: Raw cacao contains many antioxidants, which makes it an excellent purifier. It is also good for stimulating the pineal gland, the "third eye" and intuition.

Citric Acid: Squeezed lemon juice is great for detoxifying your pineal gland.

You can mix this lemon juice with spring water; it is refreshing, and it is less bad for the teeth because of less acidity.

Garlic: A garlic cure is excellent for decalcification because garlic helps dissolve calcium and acts as an antibiotic. Garlic is also good for the immune system. During your cure, increase your dose gradually to a head of garlic a day! To avoid bad breath, squeeze the garlic and mix it with apple cider vinegar or fresh lemon juice.

Boron: Boron is excellent for detoxifying and cleansing of the pineal gland. It is also effective in removing fluoride. You can try adding 1/4 teaspoon of sodium borate (borax) to your green tea. A cheap source of boron is classic borax, which can be purchased in most supermarkets. Borax should be taken in very small quantities, in pure water, with no more than 1/32 to 1/4 teaspoon of borax per liter of water. The safe and effective way is to consume this mixture in small quantities throughout the day.

Chlorella: Did you know that chlorella has a phytochemical element that can effectively rebuild nerve damage in the brain and nervous system; in this way, chlorella is used to recover patients with Alzheimer's disease and Parkinson's disease. You can live literally just by eating micro-algae like Chlorella and Spirulina; they are superfoods from 2 to 8 microns, so the size of the blood cells.

The fact that chlorella is green comes from its chlorophyll content. It does not contain refined carbohydrates, contains a high level of digestive protein, contains fatty acids, not bad fat, contains chlorophyll. It is said that chlorella is a perfect whole. In addition to being a complete protein it contains all the vitamins; B, vitamin C, vitamin E, and the main minerals (such as iron zinc in amounts large enough to be considered complimentary), it has been found, that it improves the immune system, improves digestion and detoxification; accelerate healing, protect against radiation, it helps in the prevention of degenerative diseases, helps in the treatment of disease, and relieves arthritis pain, because of its nutritional value, and helps the success of many diets to lose weight.

Zeolite: Zeolite is a mineral found in the ancient seabed and derived from volcanic rocks. Its honeycomb-shaped molecules have the ability to capture large quantities of toxins of all types safely and expel them through the urinary tract. It can be considered +++ clay. It is delivered in very fine powder obtained by a special micronization process.

For excess calcium, we will also focus on vitamin K2, which acts as a regulator of calcium in the tissues, promoting on one side the fixation of calcium in the matrix of the bones and cleaning on the other all the deposits useless.

Avoid all foods that contain pesticides: To detoxify the pineal gland, the best is to make a cure composed largely of raw fruits and vegetables, but of course, without pesticides. The meat also contains pesticides, often when the animals eat cereals or grass having have been treated. Some people recommend vegetarian diets to detoxify the body or to protect the pineal gland against potentially harmful substances. Yet some meats are still recommended, so how to manage priorities?

If you cannot pronounce the chemical name of a product, it is probably bad for your health. Among these chemicals we find:

Artificial sweeteners such as aspartame (there are slightly more natural sweeteners like xylitol).

Refined white sugar (to be replaced by brown sugar, honey, molasses, agave syrup or maple syrup, cooked wine).

Deodorants and products against bad odors, industrially produced Dental mouthwashes (replace with saltwater, enough!)

Chemical cleaning products

Activate Melatonin Production

Melatonin: Although there is no really conclusive evidence, many people believe that melatonin helps eliminate fluoride by increasing the decalcification of the pineal gland, which helps to degrade existing calcification.

To produce melatonin, our body uses an essential amino acid, tryptophan, which is extracted from the food proteins we absorb. Tryptophan is then converted to serotonin, which will itself be converted by the pineal gland into melatonin, which the liver will then metabolize. Melatonin limits oxidation in all cellular compartments, it increases the activity of other antioxidant enzymes, so it has an anti-aging effect.

Tips to Naturally Maintain a Good Level of Melatonin

Melatonin is mostly synthesized at night, and its production is stimulated by the absence of light.

At night, expose yourself as little as possible to an excess of light, which could lower or even suppress the concentration of melatonin. Even try to avoid any light source (avoid sleeping with a night light, for example). The light disrupts the production of melatonin. If you need to have a light in the hallway or the bathroom, use a light that filters the blue spectrum. (Yellow light bulbs).

The day, if you expose yourself to the sunlight, the production of melatonin at night will be favored.

Eat foods that promote the production of melatonin: melatonin is synthesized from serotonin, and this is derived from tryptophan, an essential amino acid. It is, therefore, necessary to focus on foods containing tryptophan. What are they?

Parsley, pumpkin seeds, cheese, cod, parmesan, milk and soy, turkey, pineapple, eggs, dates, lettuce, bananas, plums, rice, corn, and oatmeal, walnuts and hazelnuts, tomatoes, potatoes, and red wine are rich in tryptophans. It is, therefore, necessary to consume these foods regularly, so as to obtain an optimal serotonin level. For example, nut consumption increases blood melatonin levels in rats by a factor of three.

The Miracles of the Nettle

The forgotten nettle is a real wealth of the wild world. Its particularity is to facilitate the decristallization of the pituitary and pineal gland.

Its leaf is particularly rich in calcium, iron, boron, beta-carotene or pro- vitamin A, α-tocopherol (vitamin E) and vitamin C. In 100 grams of fresh nettle leaves, has all the recommended daily contributions of calcium and iron, as well as 6 times the RDA of pro-vitamin A and 4 times that of vitamin C. Reason for which the nettle is to be consumed rather in the morning or at midday than in the evening.

Nettle leaf also contains a large quantity of 18 different amino acids (out of 20 existing), including the 8 essential amino acids (isoleucine, leucine, lysine, methionine, phenylalanine, threonine, tryptophan and valine) necessary for the development of an organism. By comparison, cereals are all deficient in lysine (some also tryptophan), while legumes are deficient in methionine. The nettle leaf contains the 8 essential amino acids in harmonious proportions, making it a complete food.

The nettle leaf still contains, among others, chlorophyll in large quantities, silica, flavonoids (quercitin), secretin (hormone stimulating the activity of the pancreas). Some are rare components, such as choline acetyl transferase, an enzyme that synthesizes acetylcholine, and nettle is the only known plant to possess this enzyme. If one was not yet convinced of it, it is proof that the nettle is not a plant like the others.

Other Basic Methods With Which You Can Start Work on the Activation of the Pineal Gland

1. Take the maximum from night and day

For the development of the pineal gland, it is very important that the schedule of sleep and wakefulness of a person does not go astray. The most useful sleep regimen for the pineal gland is early falling asleep (around 10 pm) and early rise (ideally, at dawn).

In addition to sleeping in the dark, it is also necessary to learn how to maximize the benefits in the daytime - more often to be in the sun (or at least sit by the window).

2. Electromagnetic fields are your enemies

Electromagnetic fields haunt us everywhere: we even carry them with us in our pockets (telephones), spend leisure time and working hours with them (computers). Of course, such an impact negatively affects the development of the pineal gland, so it is so important to use every opportunity to stay away not only from the bustle of the city but also from worldly goods.

3. Meditate whenever possible

Meditation is a powerful practice that can change a person's life. It is scientifically proven that it has a beneficial effect on the state of mind and the entire human body, helping to find harmony, to know oneself, and to be distracted from the bustle. during meditation, focus your attention precisely on the pineal gland, on the Third Eye.

Meditate regularly and chant mantras. Singing causes resonance in the nose, and this resonance makes the pineal gland work. The more often it is excited, the more hormones of youth are secreted into your body. The sound "OM" resonates with the fourth chakra, known as the center of the heart, or the place of Unconditional Love. The repetition of OM opens the path to universal and cosmic consciousness. You can repeat it for 5 minutes, 10 minutes, or any other amount of time.

4. Do yoga

Yoga pays considerable attention to the development of the pineal gland since the pineal gland is considered to be the very antenna with which our brain is able to perceive the most important information from the outside. The most useful posture for the development of the pineal gland is Shashankasana, i.e., hare pose, as it stimulates the pineal gland and upper chakra. Thanks to this asana, one can also improve memory and concentration.

5. Use such aids as crystals

Amethyst, laser quartz, moonstone, purple sapphire, tourmaline, rhodonite, sodalite. In general, any natural stone of blue, indigo or purple colors can be used to activate the pineal gland, as well as work on Ajna and Sahasrara.

Take the stone and place it between the eyebrows for 15 minutes. Try to look at it with your eyes closed. Maintain a maximum concentration of these 15 minutes. It is very good if you can do this under direct access to the sun - then its rays will pass through the stone into the pineal gland. Moreover, it will be easier to concentrate on the light.

6. Use aromatic oils to stimulate the pineal gland and alleviate the general mental state

They also help with meditations and various other practices. It is recommended to use lavender, sandalwood, frankincense, pine, lotus, wormwood. Oils can be inhaled, ignited in special lamps, sprayed, or added to the bathwater.

7. Use magnets for detoxification

Just put it between your eyebrows for several hours. They attract alkali and thus remove calcium crystals from the pineal gland.

8. Forget about alcohol, nicotine, and caffeine

These stimulants interfere with the established melatonin production system. The less you consume them, the better for you and for your sleep.

Some drugs also have the ability to disrupt the production of melatonin - do not forget to consult a doctor.

9. Clear your mind at the new moon.

The new moon is considered an excellent time not only for all kinds of undertakings but also for the development of the pineal gland. If you manage to clear your mind, you will feel how the pineal gland activates and brings calm, balance to your body and cleans it. That is why in yoga, the day of the new moon is of such great importance: yogis are fully committed to spiritual practices, not being distracted even by eating food and water.

10. Make it a habit to look at the sun for 15 minutes immediately after it rises and at sunset daily.

Chapter 3 Kundalini and the Power of the Chakras

Kundalini Introduction and Overview

Kundalini is the Sanskrit word for spiritual power that resides in every person. This is the essence of the inner Self, which is also called the Holy Spirit, the Divine Light, the Divine Mother, and is

known by many other names. This is the most subtle manifestation of an inexhaustible source of energy. All people, regardless of the historical era, religion, or culture, are filled with the highest energy of kundalini. The realization of her sacred presence is the goal of all spiritual efforts. Kundalini lives in a subtle body; in a dormant state, it supports the vital functions of a person and his consciousness; the awakened kundalini leads a person to spiritual heights and helps to achieve liberation. The awakening of kundalini imposes a great responsibility on a person; from this time, he begins a new stage in his internal development. The ascension of spiritual energy becomes a pleasant process leading to holiness and enlightenment. This is how the Divine Plan of Human Development is realized.

Kundalini means "coiled," like a snake. The image of a serpent coiled up in rings is associated with infinite power, hidden power, or unused potential that each person possesses to achieve a life that is best in all respects. Another image associated with kundalini is an ocean of creative energy that rises like a tornado along the spine. Kundalini should not be thought of as some kind of alien force hostile to man. It must be perceived as creative energy, transforming consciousness.

The concept of kundalini can also be considered in a purely psychological aspect. Here it is permissible to consider it an endless source of psychic energy or gates to the world of the superconscious.

The awakening of kundalini is the beginning of spiritual enlightenment, the main step towards self-realization and enlightenment. According to the authoritative researcher Swami Prajananda, the main purpose of awakening kundalini is to help a person achieve the Divine. The awakening of inner strength becomes the beginning of the process of spiritual transformation.

To work with kundalini, it is not necessary to devote yourself to yoga or to be a Hindu or a Tibetan. Anyone can use the wisdom of spiritual science. The doctrine of kundalini is intended not only for people engaged in Eastern methods of self-realization, such as yoga. Each spiritual tradition has its own way of transmitting transcendental wisdom, using its own terminology and symbols. A study of metaphysical traditions shows that even in orthodox religious schools, there are innumerable cases of conversion to the kundalini energy.

The scientific method of research is quite applicable to the idea of kundalini. Gopi Krishna says that kundalini is the evolutionary power of consciousness and that its full development ends with the formation of a spiritual person.

Kundalini is the key to unraveling the mysteries of psychological, mental, occult, and spiritual phenomena. Its importance to people is enormous, as it offers a clue to the very secrets of life and demonstrates the capabilities of the human person.

The science of kundalini is one of the most difficult branches of yogic knowledge. To understand the meaning of the term kundalini, Swami Rama points to the need to perceive it in the context of the concept of shakti. The concept of kundalini comes from the word kadala ("folded"). As indicated above, the idea of kundalini is traditionally conveyed in the form of a coiled snake. The word shakti comes from the root of shak ("to have power," "to be able"). Together, these two Sanskrit words can be translated as "resting power."

From physics, it is known that energy exists in two forms: (1) dynamic, or active, and (2) hidden potential. Any activity or power has a static phase. When consciousness manifests itself as a creative or dynamic principle (shakti), it, in turn, polarizes itself into these two forms. With the manifestation of the Universe, part of the shakti energy becomes involved in self-manifestation, while an even larger part remains unused. The dynamic aspect is shakti in a certain differentiated form. In the Indian tradition, the main force that remains after creation is symbolized by coiled energy in the form of a snake that supports the universe. Spiritual development is a natural, universal process characteristic of any culture, era, and spiritual tradition. Such a process is associated with the development of the nature of the spirit. World religious and metaphysical traditions use various symbols and metaphors to describe the process of spiritual growth. Symbolic representations of spiritual development and experience can be found in all religions. A common ancient symbol to denote the sacred process taking place inside a person is a maze.

Why Is It Important to Learn and Practice Kundalini

Studying kundalini is an understanding of spirituality. The science and practice of studying kundalini provide an understanding of how to properly maintain and manage spiritual growth. Kundalini is only a name, a name used to denote a special field of study and practice in the ancient spiritual tradition of India. Amazing in its breadth, technical accuracy, variety of methods, and applicability, the traditional science of kundalini is a comprehensive, universal system for understanding and improving spiritual life. Kundalini is a factor that is the key to all spiritual experiences.

Based on scriptures, oral tradition, individual leadership, sociological research, and direct spiritual experience, the science of kundalini is today a powerful tool for transforming and raising consciousness.

Awakening and Ascension of Kundalini

As long as Kundalini remains in Muladhara (root and basis of existence), man is completely attached to this transitory world. But when a person carries out a religious or yoga practice, the kundalini wakes up and (although, as already mentioned, she does not sleep) begins to send energy pulses to various parts of the body through ida, pingala, Lakshmi and Sarasvati-nadi. But kundalini can fully rise only through sushumnu-nadi.

Different people are prone to different methods and ways of raising the kundalini. That is, there are different ways of raising. There are several of them.

1. Mantra japa, "chanting mantras and prayers with love and devotion."

2. The blessing of the great saints.

3. Rituals, temple worship, and bhakti.

4. The joint chanting of the name and glory of God (sankirtan).

5. Asceticism and austerities.

6. Selfless activity for the benefit of people and service to God (karma yoga).

7. Jnana Yoga.

8. Pranayama.

9. Mudras, bandhas, asanas.

10. In-depth study of the subject.

11. Other ways.

Raising kundalini is not an easy task. This can take years of hard and inspiring work. But Mother Kundalini is very supportive of determined to students and constantly gives them spiritual joys that strengthen them and illuminate their path.

Now we will consider methods, ways that contribute to raising the kundalini.

Mantra Japa

The mantra japa is the repetition of the mantra. A mantra is a power, the carrier of which is sound, audible, or inaudible. According to Vedic tradition, a mantra is a manifestation of Shabd-Brahman. The name of God is a mahamantra, a great mantra. The name of God is not different from God himself. In the divine name, all the energies of God are embodied. The mind focused on the divine name in continuous meditation, becomes divine and pure as the Divine itself. The mind accepts the qualities of the object that contemplates. This principle is the basis of religious and yogic practice.

Each letter of the Sanskrit alphabet is considered a mantra, and fifty letters are imprinted on the fifty petals of six lotuses. Of course, they are present there in a subtle and causal form. Their subtle form is called the matrix.

Mantras in all forms are manifestations of the kundalini itself. And kundalini fills the mantra with power.

Due to the constant focus on the Divine, on the glory, power, and qualities of God, the constant chanting of His name, the mind becomes pure and powerful.

If the mantra is repeated regularly and correctly, then the body, heart, mind, and nadi are purified. This facilitates the rise of Kundalini to higher planes.

The Blessing of Saints and Teachers

Thanks to the grace of the guru, a person can instantly gain all perfection. A guru is a person who owns his mind, feelings, and motives, comprehends the truth, and abides in God. Such great souls, with the help of their powers, can make the kundalini rise. For this, one glance or touching the student's body is enough. Through diksa (initiation, initiation), the true guru gives impetus to kundalini. But so that the raising of kundalini is safe and does not cause negative consequences, the student is recommended to properly prepare. For a certain time, the student is obliged to observe restrictive principles, maintain celibacy, meditate, worship the Deities, chant mantras.

All these actions purify the mind, heart, body, and nadi.

Kirtan

When people loudly with devotion chant the names, deeds, glories of God, then this is called kirtan. At the highest point of kirtan, when all thoughts are concentrated on the Beloved Lord and feelings are pulled like strings, believers forget about music and at the same time, dissolve into the music of kirtan. They begin to dance in glee.

Often the raising of kundalini is accompanied by an unexpected appearance of emotions - then the worshiper cries, laughs, trembles, or falls unconscious.

Often after kirtan and dancing, neophytes can feel a strong sexual desire. This means that the raised currents of the Kundalini descended to the sexual center. If a person does not have a purity of mind and patience, he can commit an immoral act.

An abrupt lowering of the kundalini currents is very dangerous. Because of this, many sincere aspirations for the knowledge of God ended in immorality.

Aspiration alone is not enough; spiritual knowledge and purity are required.

An ignorant attempt to raise Kundalini is like a child playing with a sharp razor. The razor is useful only in the hands of an adult who knows how to handle it.

Asceticism and austerities

Asceticism means voluntary abstinence from sensual pleasures. Asceticism and penance help a person to form character, strengthen the will, maintain mental strength and purity. Of all the ascetic feats, celibacy (brahmacharya) is the highest. This refers to the celibacy of the body, mind, and speech. A lot of valuable energy and time is wasted on sex and sensual pleasures. The cleansing of the mind and nadi with austerities and abstinence makes it possible to raise the kundalini to higher planes.

Devotional service to God and selfless activity (karma yoga)

Attachment to the fruits of activity deprives the mind of peace and binds with the bonds of karma. If a person performs all the actions, devoting the results to the Almighty, then his mind quickly finds peace, purity, and focus on Paramatma, the Supreme Spirit. All this facilitates the raising of kundalini to the higher chakras.

Here it should be said once again that without bhakti, devotion, it is impossible to achieve success by any efforts and methods.

Jnana Yoga

Jnana has two meanings: pure consciousness (svarupa) and the intellectual process of recognition (kriya jnana).

This process consists in distinguishing between what is true and what is untrue, what is Brahman and what is non-Brahman. In the process, the yogi comes to understand his true essence, the true Self.

First, the yogi asks himself the question: "Who am I?"

Then he analyzes and discards everything that is not a true Self. "I am not a body, not feelings, not objects of feelings, not will, not mind, not prana, not intelligence. These substances change and disappear. This is not I. I am spiritual; I am eternal; I have no death and birth. "

But man is not only intelligence. He has feelings and a body. Therefore, so that they do not interfere with the practice of jnana yoga, they are occupied with worship or hatha yoga. Through various methods, control over the mind, feelings, and prana is exercised. And when chitta-vritti (modifications of the mind) are eliminated, then the Supreme Spirit, Paramatma, is revealed.

Hatha Yoga

This is body cleansing. Hatha yoga includes those forms of yogic practice that relate primarily to the gross physical body. Since the physical body is associated with the subtle body, control of the physical body leads to control of the subtle body, consisting of the mind, intellect, false ego (ahamkara), feelings, and, conversely, work with subtle bodies affects the gross body.

Hatha yoga is prescribed for special individuals who, in order to control the subtle body and mind, must first master the physical body. Hatha yoga is auxiliary to other, more refined processes. The word hatha has two roots: ha and tha, which mean, respectively, "Sun" and "Moon," that is, prana and apana vayu. Practical hatha yoga consists of seven steps:

a) purification (shodhana) through six processes (shatkarma);

b) gaining strength and endurance through asanas;

c) strength and endurance (sthirata) through mudras (special positions of the body);

d) peace of mind (dhayriya) through curbing the senses (pratyahara);

e) achieving ease through pranayama;

f) self-awareness (pratyaksha) through meditation (dhyana);

g) detachment (nirliptattva) through samadhi.

Body cleansing

Those whose body is slagged and suffers from ailments and diseases are recommended to practice six cleansing exercises (shatkarma), which cleanse the body and facilitate the practice of pranayama. Such purification of the body and nadi achieves perfect health, longevity, and endurance.

Shatkarma

Shata - six, karma - action) are very effective for cleansing the body and mind. They should be performed in a clean place under the guidance of an experienced mentor.

Dhauti

This is otherwise known as throat cleansing. For such cleansing, a thin cotton cloth (such as gauze) is used with a width equal to the length of the index finger and fifteen measures long (one measure is the distance between the end of the index finger and the wrist). The fabric is moistened in warm water and slowly swallowed and then gently, quietly pulled out. On the first day, they swallow one measure of length, increasing by one measure on each subsequent day.

Dhauti practice takes fifteen days. People with diseases like phlegms can continue this practice longer. Dhauti cleanses the digestive tract, cures diseases of the bronchi, asthma, skin diseases, spleen.

Vasti

This is bowel cleansing. A tube of young soft bamboo is inserted into the anus with a length equal to the length of the middle finger and half a finger thick. The tube is oiled. Then the performer squats in the water (in the pose of Utkatasana) and draws water into the anus and then pushes it out. Repeat many times.

Vasti increases appetite, kindles a fire in the stomach, and cures dropsy, metabolic disorders, diseases of the intestinal tract, gall bladder, hemorrhoids, removes toxins.

Neti

This is nasopharyngeal cleansing. To clean the nostrils, use a piece of cord, lubricated in ghee. The end of the cord is inserted into the nostril and pulled out through the mouth, or threaded through both nostrils. Neti can be made by passing water through the nose. This is jala neti. Netty cures sinusitis, chronic runny nose, stimulates the nervous system, improves vision, and grants subtle vision.

Trataka

This is eye cleansing. Carefully, without blinking, look at some object (most often they look at the flame of a candle and the image of the Divine) until tears appear in the eyes. When tears flow, close your eyes and visualize the image.

Trataka helps with eye disease, increases the strength of concentration, gives subtle vision.

Nauli

Sequential compression and twisting of the left and right and right abdominal muscles.

Nauli stimulates gastric fire, massages internal organs, improves skin color, stimulates the nervous system.

Kapalabhati

Exercise "blacksmith furs." Inhale and exhale sharply and noisily, like blacksmith bellows. Stop as soon as you feel the tension. This exercise destroys diseases caused by excess phlegm.

In addition, there are other ways to cleanse. Ayurveda, for example, prescribes fasting as the most effective method. Three-Day fasting in warm water cleanses the body of toxins and diseases without drugs. Sometimes oshadhi yoga, that is, herbal medicine is used to cleanse.

Bandha

Bandhas (castle) are physical methods of controlling prana. The three most important of them are uddiyana, mula, and jalandhara. Thanks to the first, activated prana enters sushumna. The second connects prana and apana and directs them together into sushumna.

Mula bandha is performed like this: you need to hold the anus with your left heel, place your right foot on your left thigh, inhale and hold your breath as much as possible, then slowly exhale. During air retention, one should focus on sushumna. The usual direction for apana is down, but through compression in the region of muladhara, it goes up, where it meets prana. In this case, the internal heat in the body increases sharply, and the kundalini, sensing this, awakens from its sleep. After that, she must be sent to Sushumna.

Jalandhara bandha is performed with a deep breath. The chin is held firmly to the base of the neck.

Mahamudra

Gently squeeze the anus with the left heel, stretch the right leg, grab the fingers, inhale slowly, and hold your breath. Press the chin on the chest, fixing the look between the eyebrows. Hold this pose as much as you can, then exhale slowly. Then do the same by changing your legs. This mudra cures hemorrhoids, tuberculosis, enlargement of the spleen, gastritis, leprosy, fever, and helps to raise the kundalini. Mudras and bandha should be done regularly in the morning, after dousing, on an empty stomach.

Pranayama

The word pranayama is often translated as "breath control." But we must take into account that the word prana means not only "rough air," but also "life force." Thus, pranayama is the science of the mysterious, invisible, all- pervasive power and its management.

Cosmic higher prana manifests itself in various forms. Prana Shakti is a synonym for Kundalini Shakti, the energy of God. Prana is the subtlest substance, and it is not perceived by the senses. Prana manifests itself as gravity, like an electromagnetic field, as a life force. Breathing is just one of the functions of prana. The grossest manifestation of prana in the body is breathing.

The mind, prana, and virya (seed) are closely related. The subjugation of the mind leads to the subjugation of prana and virya. By controlling breathing, one can control prana, and controlling prana leads to controlling the mind and virya. Virya (or sukra, seed) exists throughout the body in a subtle form, and as a result of sexual desire, it goes down and is embodied in a gross, dense form in the genitals. The true brahmachari must know how to use the help of pranayama to turn the gross seed into subtle and to prevent the formation of gross seed. The body of a man who is a true urdhvareta exudes a lotus scent. If a practitioner does not strictly observe celibacy, then his practice of pranayama can lead to a fall or madness.

To perform pranayama, sit facing east or north in any position convenient for you in which you can sit for a long time without tension (but best of padmasana). The spine should be straight. Pranayama is practiced on an empty stomach, at least three hours after eating. (During pranayama, imagine that kundalini rises in sushumna.)

The place for practice should not be too remote (for example, a dense forest) so that there is no feeling of anxiety. Not intended for pranayama and the city due to the bustle and polluted atmosphere. Food should be clean and vegetarian.

Fasting is not permitted during the practice of pranayama. The yogi should not be left without food for more than one pit (3 hours). Hard work and tedious exercises should be avoided.

There are various types of pranayama, but they all serve the main purpose: to prepare the nadi, body, and mind to raise the kundalini, introduce prana into sushumna and allow it to reach the sahasrara after the Devi Kundalini, accompanied by its surroundings, various forces and pranas, passes all the lotuses - chakras.

Here I describe one pranayama that can be performed without a teacher:

Sit straight, close the right nostril with the thumb of your right hand. Inhale very slowly without noise. Fill the lungs as much as possible through the left nostril and, closing the left nostril, with the index and middle fingers of the right hand, slowly exhale through the right nostril as quietly and silently as possible.

After exhaling through the right nostril, inhale through it and exhale through the left. That will be one cycle or one pranayama. Do four such cycles without interruption. Practice this pranayama four times a day: morning, noon, evening, and midnight.

If you perform this pranayama systematically for several months, it will purify the nadi. As you inhale, think carefully that breathing fills you with strength, love, goodness, holiness, and wisdom. When exhaling, imagine that all weaknesses, vices, diseases, and desecrations leave the body and mind. During this process, try mentally pronouncing your mantra or sacred syllable OM. It spiritualizes consciousness. Thanks to the practice of pranayama, your face will become calm, enlightened, rude, and harsh features will disappear, your mind will become persistent, your voice deep and pleasant.

But pranayama is a preliminary step in laya yoga or kundalini yoga. To raise the kundalini, daily practice is prescribed, which most often takes years of hard work, although in exceptional cases, success is achieved in a relatively short time. In the beginning, kundalini can be raised to the lower centers. The one who brought her to a center next time easily reaches this level. But, to go higher, further persistent efforts are required. Upon reaching each center, the practitioner experiences a special kind of bliss and acquires special powers. However, in the very early stages, Shakti has a tendency to return.

Constant practice eliminates the possibility of spontaneous return back. A perfect yogi is able to keep Shakti in sahasrara for as long as he wishes.

The Health Benefits of Kundalini

While there are several benefits of kundalini, I outline ten basic points for self-improvement, which are easily achieved with regular classes in this spiritual and physical practice.

1.) Benefits for all body systems

Kundalini helps to cope with migraines, problems in the functioning of food systems, headaches, and also puts in order the hormonal, genitourinary, endocrine, cardiovascular, and other body systems.

2.) Gives beauty

Despite the fact that practice belongs to the category of sedentary, it is quite possible to achieve a beautiful, developed and harmonious body with it. Due to the fact that kundalini charges from the inside, this inner radiance also affects the appearance. In addition, it normalizes hormonal processes, which in turn has a positive effect on the appearance and psyche.

3.) Charges with power

For some, the essence of strength lies in physical superiority, while some consider strengthing a character's resistance to stressful situations. Kundalini will provide you with both of them, and will also help you feel in harmony with your body, give peace of mind and peace of mind.

4.) The joy of life

It is very difficult for someone who does not know how to relax to see the positive aspects of life. The self-confidence, peace, and spiritual component that the kundalini gives will help you find gaps even in the most critical situations and enjoy every day.

5.) Promote emotional balance

Thanks to kundalini, you will cease to react sharply to trifles that are not worth your attention, you will be able to quickly make decisions and immediately migrate to actions, as well as be able to control your emotions and prevent their unreasonable splash.

6.) Heightened perception

Many things will be revealed to you on the other, true side. Kundalini yoga will allow you to more clearly feel what is happening around and give events a sober assessment.

7.) Reveals the sixth sense

Kundalini exercises affect the areas of the brain that are responsible for intuition. So, now you can easily make decisions in contentious issues, relying on the sixth sense.

8.) Helps to break a bad habit

Yoga itself becomes your main habit and carries the philosophy of cleansing the soul and body of things that can harm you.

9.) Unleashes creativity

Due to the increase in energy and activity, you will want to try yourself in new areas all the time, which implies that the use of kundalini is also in the disclosure of unknown talents.

10.) Spiritual development

You will begin to look at life differently, learn to make efforts to improve living conditions, and stop being upset over trifles.

Chapter 4 Kundalini: Practical Tips and Notes

Then kundalini first enters sushumna, there will be great pain. Many are afraid of these pains, mistakenly believing that this is caused by some kind of disease. When kundalini fully

enters sushumna, the activities of the major nadi freeze. Then prana and the emanations of kundalini pass only through sushumna. The passage of kundalini shakes the whole body like an unexpected shock from an earthquake.

The scriptures speak of various ways of promoting kundalini, depending on the element (tattva) prevailing in a person.

This is a movement similar to the movement of an ant — a movement like a frog jumping on lotuses. The movement of the kundalini is felt like the movement of a wriggling snake. The movement is similar to a bird flight. It is perceived in the region of the heart and is accompanied by a feeling of flight and lightness. Kundalini jumps from one center to another, flying two or three in a row. A movement like a monkey jumping from branch to branch. Shakti can "slip through" three or four chakras.

If the emanations of kundalini began to rise along Sarasvati or Lakshmi- nadi, they should be lowered through meditation to muladhara and sent to sushumna.

Clearing Out Negative Energy

Yoga teachers prescribe the following method for this. It should be performed on an empty stomach. Sit cross-legged. Inhale slowly through both nostrils. Pull the lower abdomen towards the spine and up. Squeeze the anus and slowly lead the kundalini up, presenting it as light, energy, or a luminous Goddess. Throughout the path of movement, mentally follow her ascent. When you lead it to the soma chakra, exhale, relax the stomach and muscles of the anus.

At first, imagination and suggestion are necessary, but after a long practice, you can really raise the kundalini to the higher centers.

Start with three minutes in the morning and evening, gradually increasing the time to half an hour.

Through systematic practice, one can easily eliminate negative energy, turning it into ojas (psychic energy), and strengthen meditation. After exercise, it is recommended to drink cow's milk.

Blockages That Prevent Kundalini from Rising Smoothly, and How to Clear These Blockages

All sorts of currents, impulses, emanations come from the kundalini; most of them exit through the anus and genital canal. In order to close these channels, ascetics and sannyasis wear a kaupin, a tight loincloth.

With the loss of seed during intercourse, a tremendous loss of energy is produced by the Kundalini Shakti. Strictly observe celibacy; otherwise, the practice of yoga will be useless to you and even dangerous. For a family man seeking spiritual perfection, sexual relations are permissible only for the purpose of conceiving children.

It is said that the energy spent during one sexual intercourse is equal to the energy spent on physical work within 24 hours. If energy is not wasted on sexual pleasures, then a person gains a strong memory, a strong will, a powerful mind, and moral purity. The scriptures say that loss of seed brings physical death closer. If a man often engages in sexual relations, then he becomes irritable, weak, painful, his memory and will weaken, his intellect becomes dulled. He becomes a toy in the hands of low passions.

You should completely abandon the use of alcohol, drugs, and tobacco. These substances pollute the nadis, make the mind restless, feelings, uncontrollable, and excite low passions. He who smokes and performs pranayama is a suicide. Even tea and coffee have a stimulating effect on the mind and therefore interfere with concentration.

Eat right. Avoid unclean, stale, indigestible, and poorly prepared foods. Eliminate meat, fish, and eggs from your diet. Do not take any food or drink from the hands of immoral, depraved people. Such food is contagious. As you take precautions when dealing with people with tuberculosis, cholera, or plague for your physical health, you should also take precautions for spiritual and mental health. If you do not pay serious attention to this, you will suffer, and your spiritual progress will be complicated. Mental emanations and karma are included in food, especially in legumes during cooking on a fire. That is why the yogis of India have established very strict rules regarding food. And this is not superstition. Try to cook for yourself and eat only consecrated food, so you will avoid many traps and dangers. After preparation, offer it to God by reading prayers, mantras. It will sanctify food.

Fill the stomach halfway with food, a quarter with water, leave a quarter empty.

Control your speech. Say only that which brings spiritual benefit to you and others. Speak calmly and softly, avoid rude and deceitful words. Be silent for one day, and you will see how much energy is saved.

Do not get carried away with healing with the help of prana (or a biofield, as many say). This is associated with a risk to life and spiritual practice.

When a person acquires a certain purity of body, nadi, and mind, he can easily heal, but the subsequent reaction will be dangerous. Often the healer takes on the disease of the person he cured. At first, he will successfully heal people, but after several successful cures, he will fail and begin to suffer from incurable diseases and life troubles. Many engaged in such healing, for vanity or for show, end up with mental and bodily diseases, unbelief, and apathy. To get rid of the negative effects of healing, you must have great spiritual strength and know how to neutralize unwanted reactions.

When the kundalini reaches anahata, the yogi can hear various sounds emanating from anahata that help to achieve a state of deep meditation: birds chirping, shell sound, guilt, mridanga, flute, pakhawaja (drum type), lion roar, cricket sounds, bell ringing, pipe sounds.

Visions depend on the student's inclinations and intensity. All this is given only for encouragement or verification, but no more. But some foolish people create a lot of noise around these phenomena. They are vain with their small achievements, advertise themselves, try to find students, but pride and vanity take away all the fruits. To keep followers around themselves, they go on deceit and fraud and unscrupulously use the trust of simple-minded people in order to enjoy power over souls. Because of these scammers, people lose faith in religion.

For meditation on the twelve-petalled Anahata lotus, it is recommended to repeat the twelve-syllable mantra OM NAMO BHAGAVATE VASUDEVAYA (Om. I worship the all-pervading Lord Vasudeva).

Lotus petals are numbered by the number of working energies in this chakra and by the number of nadis that are found there. These energies are controlled by different deities. (To work successfully with the chakras, one must read with the mantra and mentally worship all the deities.) By worshiping the Supreme God, Bhagavan, all demigods can be satisfied.

There are fifty mantra buckets in different parts of the body, and there are fifty different kinds of energy. There are fifty letters in the Sanskrit alphabet. The letters are imprinted on the lotus petals in a causal form, and when these sounds or letters are properly pronounced, they vibrate with the letters on the petals, causing the corresponding energies to act.

Be careful when working with kundalini currents and emanations. If they do not function properly, then this can cause illness. These currents can be controlled with the help of concentration of the mind, meditation, massage, exposure to acupuncture points, cleansing procedures, working with the sun and fire, special mantras, medicinal herbs, pranayama, proper nutrition. These methods are described in detail in Ayurveda, yogic medicine, Tibetan, and Chinese schools of working with subtle body energies, such as the qigong school.

Many practitioners of kundalini yoga and other types of yoga can manifest various ailments and disorders. Not understanding the reasons for their occurrence, they go to doctors and healers, who most often instead of treatment and relief, only complicate the situation.

There is simple pranayama available to everyone, regardless of gender and age. If it is performed in the morning and evening for a long time, it can regulate the work of currents and heal even chronic diseases. It must be performed on an empty stomach, in a clean, calm place. You can sit in any comfortable position, keeping your spine straight.

Inhale through both nostrils, squeeze the throat and force the air to collect in the upper part of the lungs, slightly pressing the stomach up and to the spine. Hold your breath as much as possible, then exhale slowly and carefully through the right nostril and inhale again through both nostrils and, holding your breath as before, exhale again through the right nostril. Exhale through the right nostril for 5 minutes, and then through the left 5 minutes. You can bring the cycle time of this pranayama to one hour. This pranayama drives out laziness, drowsiness, lack of will, passivity, fatigue, sublimation of sexual energy to the highest is achieved, the nadis are purified, the mind calms down.

Below the anahata chakra, there is an eight-petalled lotus in which Ishta Devata, the chosen Deity, is worshiped. For meditation on this lotus, the eight-syllable mantra OM NAMO NARAYANAYA is used. In this center, as stated in the Hamsa Upanishad, there is atma (individual soul) and Paramatma (Supreme Soul).

Sometimes the passage of the kundalini through various centers is considered a metaphor that reflects the path of the soul through different

planes of being and consciousness. But the experience of yogis and scriptures shows that this is far from a complete understanding.

The negative consequences arising from the practice of pranayama, layaya yoga, and other methods can be prevented and corrected by mahamantras, that is, mantras containing the name of God. Such mantras themselves correct some miscalculations in practice. Anyone who systematically repeats them will be able to get rid of three types of suffering, find love for God and all beings and achieve self-realization.

The awakening of kundalini occurs suddenly and gives rise to a surge of love in a person, which encourages him to perform wonderful actions. The sages of India say that before awakening the kundalini, you need to free the central channel of the spine - sushumna - with a clean life and appropriate exercises. Such purification is necessary for spiritual growth because when the kundalini snake awakens, it begins to activate the whole mental life of a person; it's such an intense fire that it burns everything. Therefore, the path of kundalini should be free from all impurities and all obstacles, so that it can pass it quickly and without harm to humans. The system of work with the subtle energy of the human body helps to get physical and spiritual compensation for all the tensions encountered in life, so we can be healthy.

Chapter 5 Signs of Awakening Kundalini

Each experience of climbing kundalini is unique. In each case, there is its own set of criteria. In addition, signs of the awakening of internal energy can undergo significant changes, even in the same

person. Nevertheless, there are some typical signs that indicate that a person feels the ascent of kundalini. We will consider them in this chapter. Some people who have experienced the awakening of the kundalini energy simply do not know what to do next. There are clear and unmistakable signs of the awakening of inner strength. First, trembling usually runs through the body, and gradually, a feeling of higher pleasure spreads. Then the temperature rises - this is a sign that kundalini passes through a certain energy center. In various parts of the body, foci of fire appear to appear; the whole body is sweating. Sometimes it seems

In any case, when the kundalini awakens, a person feels something rising up the spine. It's not necessary to feel the burning liquid: sometimes, it really looks like a snake crawling. As the awakened energy passes through the chakras, a person can spontaneously begin to perform yoga mudras, bandhas, or breathing exercises. Kundalini acts as a spiritual principle, guiding and leading a person along the path of enlightenment.

When energy goes up, difficulties can arise. From time to time, she can remain for a while in one chakra and even come back. There are three granthi (nodes) through which energy passes with difficulty. When kundalini penetrates the abdominal node, pain, or physical disruption of the body can be felt. The adept will most likely have to repeat the process of awakening the kundalini repeatedly, gradually moving it higher and higher. Raising the kundalini to the anahata chakra in the region of the heart is the most difficult task. It is believed that at this point of kundalini, a cycle passes from infancy to adulthood.

It is easy to awaken the kundalini, but it is very difficult to bring it to sahasrara through all the chakras. This requires a lot of patience, perseverance, purity of thought, and sustainable practice.

As the kundalini passes through the chakras, exciting them, a person observes specific visions and hears special sounds. He passes through the corresponding locks (cosmic plans). In mystical insights, each chakra corresponds to a lotus flower. When energy enters the chakra, the petals open.

The quality of the chakra, or its power, is expressed in the form of the corresponding deity. The Vedic tradition says that in Sahasrara, there is a union of Shiva and Shakti. This is the most transcendental and blissful state of consciousness. Individual consciousness merges with the Divine.

If you hold the kundalini at this point for longer than twenty-one days, the physical body will lose support and begin to disintegrate. However, it is usually very difficult to maintain such a state of consciousness, and the kundalini again returns to the lower chakra. Gradually, through systematic practice, the adept learns the art of controlling the energy of the kundalini and acquires the ability to control its movement at will, maintaining the state of consciousness that is most useful at this time.

As a preparation, it is useful to first study the anatomy of the human body, as well as gain control over the four aspirations (for food, sleep, sex, and self-preservation). You must have a healthy body and fully control your mind, actions, and speech. The mind cannot be allowed to fall under anyone's influence. Achieving all of this can take quite a while.

A sick body and a restless mind cannot work with kundalini energy. A healthy body and mind are two essential tools for awakening consciousness.

Exercises that are traditionally used to cleanse the body in preparation for awakening kundalini can also be used to improve health. However, it is wrong to apply powerful practices aimed at actively awakening internal energy with the goal of simply improving well-being.

How to Awaken a Dormant Kundalini

Here are the most important body cleansing methods required when working with a dormant kundalini.

Alternating Nostril Breathing (nadi shodhana)

- Reinforced expiration (kapalabhati) - Sit down. Exhale all the air from the lungs, take half a breath, and then take quick rhythmic exhalations through the nostrils. Accentuate each exhalation; inhalation occurs automatically. Concentrate on the ajna chakra between the eyebrows. Close your eyes and "look" them into the area of the third eye. This exercise clears the head area.

Fire extinguishing in the abdomen (agnisara dhauti) - Sit down. Put your palms on your knees, fingers facing each other. Bend your elbows a bit. Exhale all the air from the lungs and during exhalation, make rapid rhythmic movements of the abdomen back and forth. After that, gently inhale.

Brand of a horse (ashwini mudra) - Sit down. Take a deep breath. Perform fast and strong sphincter contractions.

Do these techniques daily.

Positive Thinking Power

There are all kinds of courses that teach kundalini yoga, mainly emphasizing its health benefits and not touching on the discussion of spiritual issues. In this way, hatha yoga is often taught in the West. It all depends on the attitude of the student. The desire to improve health is certainly laudable, but the awakening internal energy will gradually burn the ego, and a person who seeks to recover using the methods of kundalini yoga, is driven primarily by egocentric motives. Thus, internal tension is created, which can lead to a serious mental disorder.

The next stage of preparation is gaining perfect control over unconscious acts, as well as the central nervous system. During intense sadhana, one should observe perfect calm and also adhere to a certain diet. The stillness of the body and mind are two important signs of progress.

Ancient yogis depicted the development of humanity and human consciousness, in particular, as a sequence of seven steps. Seven centers are symbolically associated with the spinal column. These centers have already been mentioned above: these are chakras or lotuses. The word chakra, as mentioned above, means "wheel" and symbolizes the process of life. Slowly opening lotus, rooted in the mud, symbolizes the development from primitive consciousness to high. Chakras can be understood as levels of consciousness.

Since each chakra controls one of the five senses, the adherent must strive to develop each feeling as fully as possible and bring them all into balance. This will give him a significant advantage when working with internal energy.

Increase Mind Power

An ancient tradition says that all human actions originate in the mind. Energy is mostly neutral and takes shape as a result of the impact on it of thoughts, speech, and actions. The pollution of the chakras (levels of consciousness) occurs due to desires, selfishness, and scanning of the lower layers of consciousness. At the beginning of work on oneself, it is very difficult to abandon an entrenched system of beliefs and illusions. The need to perceive new information contrary to the usual beliefs seems unnecessarily brutal and even hurts. But any pain is caused by ignorance. A person believes that he is a victim of circumstances, while he actually creates for himself a shell of ignorance that prevents him from enjoying life. The practice of awakening kundalini leads to a proper perception of reality - instead of a false one that causes pain and suffering.

The Effects of Kundalini Activation on the Body, Emotions and the Mind

Seven signs are observed that are observed during the awakening of kundalini.

1. Pranic movements, or kriya

Prana is the Sanskrit word for life energy. When an energy flow moves through the body, clearing physiological blocks in its path, a person may experience involuntary cramps, twitches, muscle contractions. He can also clearly recall long-forgotten events, as well as moments from past incarnations.

The involuntary reactions and actions caused by the rise of the kundalini are kriya. Kriyas are designed to eliminate energy blocks within the spinal column. Kriyas also purify the mind. Blocks, known as samskaras, not only impede the movement of the kundalini, but they embody bindings, false notions, and other derivatives of ignorance that restrict freedom of consciousness. If you do not pay attention to material attachments, they lead to actions that make blocks in mind more and more insurmountable.

For example, if a person is attached to anger, then he will manifest it everywhere, even in situations that, it would seem, do not provoke aggression at all. With an increase in kundalini, it interacts with the matrix of anger, it purifies it, as a result of such purification, the corresponding kriya will occur. This can be compared with how a person's high temperature during an illness indicates an ongoing internal fight against infection. Such a perception of the kundalini as some kind of rational force may seem a little mystical, but, nevertheless, the mechanism of its action is just that.

Spoken language has many phrases with figurative meanings that reflect the state of mind. For example, about a person who has lost firm convictions, they say: "He has a confused mind." On the sincere - on the contrary: "This is a direct person." These phrases reflect a subtle understanding of the value of a human being. What seems like a good metaphor actually reflects the internal structure of the human body. Take a garden hose with which to water. If the hose is straight, then water will run along with it easily and freely. Another thing if the hose is tangled: if you turn on the water, there may even be a situation where the flow of water will be blocked, and the hose will swell in one place, unable to cope with the voltage. It can even break through. To some extent, a human being can be likened to such a hose. Kundalini rises quickly and freely along with the "direct" person; nothing holds it back. If a person is entangled in internal contradictions, there is no need to talk about a successful awakening of internal strength.

2. Yogic phenomena

Some people begin to perform yoga asanas, mudras, bandhas, which they never knew before or could not do in a normal state of consciousness. They can also pronounce Sanskrit words or sounds, hear internal music, sounds, mantras. In sacred Hindu texts, the kundalini is sometimes called Vak, the goddess of speech, perhaps because the awakened kundalini increases creativity and improves self-expression through speech. Changes also apply to breathe: it can accelerate or slow down greatly. Some people may not breathe at all for a long time.

3. Physiological signs

The awakening of kundalini often causes unusual physiological activity, as the intense movement of energy releases toxins in the body. A person may experience pain in the heart, head, and spine, digestive problems, and impaired functioning of the nervous system. Inner fever can lead to involuntary orgasms.

4. Psychological stress

Spiritual awakening challenges the consciousness of the ego. This leads to the loss of habitual mental balance. The consciousness of the ego leaves the center of the soul. A person enters into inexplicable emotional states unfamiliar before. Emotional outbursts range from feelings of anxiety, guilt, and depression to compassion, love, and joy.

5. Extrasensory experiments

As perceptions expand, people experience atypical visual phenomena, such as seeing lights, symbols, objects, or pictures from past lives. Audio phenomena may consist of hearing voices, music, internal sounds, or mantras. Even the olfactory system can begin to be sharply stimulated, and a person will begin to feel the scent of sandalwood. There may be a violation of the entire perceptual system of the body, ending with disorientation in space.

6. Mental phenomena

With the disclosure of mental abilities, a person can feel the visionary, telepathic, psychokinetic, healing abilities.

7. Mystical states of consciousness

A person can move into altered states of consciousness, where he directly feels the unity underlying the world. At the same time, he experiences a deep peace and clarity of awareness of cosmic wisdom.

In some cases, the changes caused by psychological stress are so acute that the behavior of a person becomes similar to the behavior of a mentally ill person.

What Can Be Done to Maintain the Awakened Kundalini?

When the awakening of kundalini happens to people who are not on the spiritual path of development or who are unable to realize the importance of the overturn of their mind, body, and spirit, such an experience can seriously damage their health. The question may arise: if kundalini is the Divine energy contained in a person, then why does its awakening cause some inconvenience?

All inconveniences associated with the ascent of kundalini are associated with flaws in the human subtle body. These flaws are caused by past injuries, improper lifestyles, or improper spiritual practices that weaken or damage the subtle organs, create energy blocks in the path of kundalini. A person cannot know the causes of these difficulties. All inconveniences are caused not by kundalini, but by mistakes made by the man himself. However, these errors can be corrected.

It is important not to confuse the awakening of kundalini with enlightenment. Enlightenment rarely follows from a separate experience with the supernatural. Usually, it is associated with the expansion of consciousness, which was somehow prepared for this. The intensity and duration of each enlightenment experience depend on the person's willingness to withstand them. The awakening of kundalini is not the endpoint of spiritual development, but the beginning of a transformation of consciousness. At the same time, no other technique is known than kundalini yoga, which would lead to enlightenment just as quickly.

In some people, the awakening of kundalini can be delayed for several years, even with intensive spiritual practice. It is worth noting here that the experience of mystical practices is already quite valuable in itself, regardless of whether it culminates in signs of ascending kundalini energy or not.

No one knows which impetus leads to the unfolding of spiritual potential. For some people, spiritual growth is a very delicate process that takes place over many years, devoted to prayers or meditations under the guidance of an experienced guru. Others may experience a sharp awakening of inner strength without even realizing how to work with it further.

Kundalini Climbing - Awakening Your Higher Self

According to traditional views, there are several ways in which kundalini can rise. These paths are characterized by different levels at which kundalini may linger. Thus, we can talk about the types of ascension of kundalini. This type is determined by external circumstances, the characteristics of the subtle body of the individual during the ascent. The quality of ascent is also influenced by such factors as a person's usual behavior, lifestyle, and general mental and emotional mood. Some people are already born with awakened kundalini. It is the merit of their spiritual practice in past lives.

So, in the aspect of raising the kundalini, the following categories are distinguished:

1.) No climbing occurs - This is a sign that the kundalini remains in a dormant state in the Muladhara Chakra. This is the state of an ordinary person.

2.) The awakening of kundalini - It can happen by chance within the muladhara chakra itself when stimulating vayu. Kundalini is unwound and reeled up without going beyond the root chakra.

3.) Kundalini release - Kundalini begins its ascent. This occurs under certain conditions.

4.) Partial ascents - Such fluctuations in internal strength are extremely unstable, the kundalini moves up and down the sushumna, sometimes reaching the anahata chakra at the level of the heart. In some people, it even reaches the chakra of the throat vishuddha.

5.) Indirect ascents - They are also unstable; the kundalini moves up and down the vajra-nadi or sarasvati-nadi. These two energy channels do not lead to the climax of the bindu, so the kundalini should be sent to sushumna.

6.) Intermediate ascents - They occur through sushumna-nadi to the level of vishuddhi chakra or even to the ajna chakra. These are steady ascents, as kundalini remains at the achieved level.

7.) Complete ascent - It occurs through sushumna-nadi (occasionally through chitrini-nadi) to the ajna chakra at the point of makara. After this, the kundalini enters the sahasrara chakra and brahma-randhra but still remains below the bindu point. At this level, completely spiritual life begins, and complete purification of consciousness takes place.

A complete ascent to the point of bindu, located at the end of the brahma- nadi above the brahma-randhra, the top of sahasrara. This is the culmination of an increase in inner strength, but not the final stage of spiritual development. A prerequisite is a fine cleaning of the body.

8.) Advanced ascent - involves the ascent and descent of the kundalini. This is the goal of the path of spiritual development. A person at this level can attain holiness and achieve final liberation, the complete union of the soul with God.

The goal of learning to die correctly is to investigate the nature of a non-physical posthumous state. It is recognized that consciousness is the ultimate reality and that it seeks to be structured on various planes of being, traditionally called in the Western tradition astral, etheric, causal, and so on. These structures are populated by entities, often described as beings of light, or angels. Many people who have experienced an out-of-body state talk about them. The beings of light, as claimed in occult and spiritual traditions, help the process of birth, entry into the world of higher consciousness.

Chapter 6 Mindfulness Meditation Higher levels of consciousness

The higher the released energy flows, the greater the spiritual uplift the meditator feels. Fire sparks emanating from the mouth of the kundalini snake reach the hemispheres of the brain, stimulating

them more and more to vigorous activity. The meditator begins to experience the deepest ecstasy, joy, and peace. It seems that the whole body is plunged into an ocean of happiness and bliss.

With the stimulation of the right hemisphere, hidden possibilities of extrasensory perception, such as clairvoyance, clairaudience, telepathy, providence, and so on, come to the surface. Consciousness begins to expand and go beyond its borders, opening up new dimensions of cosmic unity. The sense of self-identity begins to make quantum leaps into the ever-increasing orbits of the cosmic mind. This stage of comprehension of time and space is a reward to the adept for all his efforts.

Here are a few meditations that help rise to higher levels of consciousness and control internal energy.

Meditation on the clouds of light

Find a comfortable place to relax. Let your thoughts flow freely, come, and go; you are only an observer. Take a deep breath, hold your breath. Check for tension in the body. If you find such areas, free them - and on the exhale to get rid of everything that prevents you from completely relaxing. Take a deep breath again. As you exhale, release all energy and all your thoughts from the body. Take a deep breath. Feel new energy entering the body; you literally breathe in new possibilities and allow the body to become light. Relax more and more - until you stop feeling the body.

When fully relaxed, imagine a colorful mist vibrating around you. You yourself, being light, smoothly pass into this fog, just your being has a slightly higher density. Clouds of energy slowly float around you. Relax on one of them, feel safe. This cloud lifts you up and takes you to an infinite world. The boundaries between time and space are erased. You are immersed in a world of infinite beauty and endless possibilities. You are floating in the cloud, feeling how light you have become. Suddenly you see a giant rock below; the cloud softly and easily lands, you descend on a rock.

Feel the strength of the stone, feel the power emanating from the rock. You look back, and you see a big river. You cannot make out where it begins and where it ends. You are fascinated by the water stream. It is an endless river of energy, a river of life. You come closer to the water and try to examine its color, to feel it with your whole being. What sounds do you hear? You are the light, so you can safely enter the water, cross it, rush along with the stream, and when you want, stop.

Relax and try to realize what you need most at the moment. What is your main intention? What emotions will accompany you on the way to the chosen goal? Feel the energy of these emotions, feel how it moves through your light body, burns, pulsates. Inhale energy with your whole being. Try to see the paintings, images, symbols associated with it: they will appear in front of the inner eye themselves; you can only focus on them.

When you are completely filled with this energy, enter the river, dissolve for a moment in it, purify the energy, and then release it into the water. See how the energy cloud comes out of you, touches the water, and gradually disappears in the stream. Take a deep breath. Your desire merges with the source of life. Enjoy the river of life for some more time. Take a deep breath again and exit the river. Notice that the colored fog surrounds you again, and you rise up with it. You descend to the cloud and return. With each deep breath, you return to the outside world and feel peace and satisfaction.

Sacred Space Meditation

Relax, sit in a comfortable position. Close your eyes, calm your mind. Breathe slowly and deeply; breathing comes from the diaphragm. For a while, just breathe and pay attention to the spine. It is a pillar connecting earth and heaven.

Feel the energy being concentrated at both ends of this pillar. Let the flow of earthly energy move upward, exit the crown of the head, and disperse into the Universe. Together with the energy flow, all negative emotions, pain, anxiety, tension are carried away.

Your whole being is filled with peace. Let the mind be like the ocean, and thoughts - bubbles appearing on the surface of the water. You may remember your thoughts better, but for now, remain a simple observer. Breathe deeper, gradually slow down your breathing. With each breath, relax your body and mind more and more.

Feel the cool red fog enveloping you. It is not hot, not cold: you can only feel it with your skin.

Feel yourself on a cloud firm enough to hold you on yourself, but very cozy and comfortable. Each part of your body rests on a cloud: legs, arms, back, neck, head - all organs feel calm. The cloud begins to plunge slowly into the red fog, and you plunge with it. Immersion is very slow; you go deeper and deeper and relax even more. The fog begins to change its color: from brilliant red to red-orange.

Gradually, the orange color changes to yellow-lemon. Your body is also painted in lemon color. You are floating on a cloud that carries you to the green summer lawn. You can even hear the wind shaking the grass, feel the flowing blue light from heaven.

Blue light turns into purple; moonless night comes, dark, peaceful, quiet. The cloud you were floating on gently lands.

The fog disappears. You lie on your back on the green grass. You feel light blows of the wind; you can hear the faint chatter of night insects.

Wherever you are, there is always something that pulls you toward you. It may be someplace, person, impression. What you are thinking about may appear right next to you because you are in a sacred place of fulfillment of desires. Everything can change here, but any changes will occur only at your request. You yourself built this place, inhabited it. Rise, explore the sacred space in which you are. May you meet with something (or about whom) have long dreamed of.

After a while, you yourself will realize that the time has come to leave the sacred place. Say goodbye to what you saw, leave without regret, because you can always come back here whenever you want.

Lie on your back and again feel the fog enveloping you. This time it is dark, like a moonless sky. Feel the cloud again under your feet, arms, back, neck, head. It supports you - and begins to rise very slowly.

Breathe deeply, watch the gradual change of colors: the dark color of the sky turns into blue, cyan, green, yellow. All this time, you continue to rise slowly; yellow turns to summer orange, then red. Let your mind still float, and your body will slowly return to the tangible world. You begin to feel the floor with your back, to realize the room in which you are. You are coming back.

Understanding the Benefits of a Strong Meditation Practice

The mindfulness movement is rapidly gaining popularity in the Western world. If before meditation was practiced only by people who are fond of various kinds of spiritual practices, now it is considered the most common thing.

Now in Europe and here in the USA, the phrase "I practice meditation" no longer causes a wary-detached attitude, as before. So what's the point? What are some of the benefits of meditation or mindfulness? Why are more and more people doing it? I will try to answer these questions in this chapter. But let's take it in order.

What Meditation Is

In 2007, a study was published that experimentally confirmed the previously existing hypothesis that a person has two different forms of self- consciousness, and different parts of the brain are responsible for them. These two forms of self-awareness are called the narrative mode (story mode, narrative mode of self-reference), and the experience mode (empirical mode, experiential mode of self-reference).

The narrative mode is a mechanism by which we can think about the past, present, and future. Its essence is that our attention is partially or completely captured by thoughts that give meaning to what is happening. The story mode is responsible for our understanding of who we are, what is happening around us, what we are striving for, what connects us with others, and so on. The story mode connects the past, present, and future for us into one semantic picture.

The empirical mode is the ability to perceive our direct experience, what is happening to us at this second. Our direct experience consists of several parts. This is, firstly, the sensations realized with the help of the senses (hearing, sight, touch, smell, taste, balance). Secondly, these are internal sensations - thoughts, imagination, emotions, and internal states.

Meditation is the training of attention. When we meditate, we train to keep our focus on exactly what we are experiencing at the moment. That is, we train to be in the mode of experience.

Why Do We Need Each of These Forms of Self-Awareness?

Both forms of self-awareness are necessary. Narrative mode serves to perform any action. To do something, you need to make a decision. To make a decision, you need to somehow explain to yourself what is happening. Medicine knows cases of damage to the part of the brain that is responsible for the narrative regimen. In cases where this department completely loses its working capacity, a person turns into a vegetable. He does nothing more and does not say anything.

Once I read about one case when such a person fell into the pool and drowned. He could not have a motive to perform any actions for his salvation. In order for a motive to appear, one must first give the event some meaning. If the narrative mode does not work, what is happening seems pointless.

The empirical regime allows us to be in the present moment and feel what is happening to us. In addition to the fact that we get complete satisfaction from any pleasant sensations (for example, the pleasure of eating, music, sex, etc.), we are better aware of what is happening around us. That is, we can give the event meaning more accurately. The empirical mode allows us to adjust how we explain what is happening, taking into account what is happening here and now.

If the empirical regime is poorly trained, then our thoughts are more based on our ideas about ourselves and the world and to a lesser extent, on what is happening here and now.

Let's look at an example:

Victor works in sales. He is new to this business. He attended several trainings where he was told the theory. But he is not good at applying this theory in practice. When he speaks with the client, usually at some point, the client begins to close, and the contact disappears. Victor began to practice meditation. Now he notices that the contact disappears when he begins to feel excitement amid a desire to close the deal as soon as possible. Gradually, he began to recognize this sensation at an early stage and learned to behave more calmly, despite the excitement. Over time, he noticed that he began to feel more relaxed.

In this example, the practice of meditation helps Victor to pay attention to his feelings during a conversation with a client. This led to the fact that he understood the reason for the disappearance of contact with the client. As a result, over time, he first managed to adjust his behavior, and then his emotional reactions became adequate.

Awareness is a kind of feedback mechanism that allows you to adjust behavior. Without realizing what we feel, we usually act on autopilot.

Yet another example:

Andrew is a conflict person in terms of his personality. When he was angry, he could not stop. The conflict simply unwound according to a previously known scenario. But Andrew never thought about it. Each time he drew conclusions for himself and lived on. Conclusions usually came down to the fact that the other side is to blame.

When Andrew began to practice meditation, first of all, it helped him realize that he was behaving aggressively. Then he noticed that often in a conflict, he doesn't react to the essence of the issue, but to the form in which the other side answers him. This allowed him to react less emotionally. Andrew realized that from time to time, he spoke stingy, offensive phrases, the purpose of which was to offend another person. He began to learn to stop in time. The practice of mindfulness helps Andrew more often and faster turn off the autopilot in a conflict and do something for a peaceful resolution of the situation.

What Other Benefits Does Meditation Provide?

The fact is that the mechanisms of attention are the most low-level mechanisms of our consciousness. Therefore, the practice of meditation affects absolutely all aspects of our lives. Known and research-confirmed effects include:

- Increased attention span. Reducing the number of random distractions.
- Improving self-control ability.
- Increasing the pain threshold.
- Improving learning and memorization.
- Reduces irritability and stress.

Meditation to Attain Your Divine Self

As you have seen in the mediation guides, the most common meditation technique is observing breathing. Despite the fact that it is very good for training concentration, in terms of awareness of your divine self, you need to take it up a notch. For this, I recommend trying a technique called marking or mental noting.

Marking is a technique from the attention category without a choice. In other words, we are not trying to concentrate on something specific, but simply try to notice what is happening to us, whatever that is. And when we notice, we call it one word. Perhaps we feel some sensations in the body. Perhaps we are thinking about something. Maybe we want something. Maybe we imagine something. Anything. In a word.

There are various marking options without a choice. You can start with anyone. The easiest option is to use only three words: see, hear, feel. Moreover, each word can refer to both external sensation and internal. For example, the word "hear" can denote perception by the hearing organs and the thought that "sounds" in the head. As for the time for meditation, 10-15 minutes a day is enough to start. It is advisable to find the time when no one will bother you.

While meditating, you can sit, lie, stand, or walk. Eyes may be open or closed. You can sit on a chair or on the floor. All this is not so important at first. It is important to remember that the practice of meditation is a long game. And therefore, at the first stage, it is advisable not to overdo it.

The practice of meditation is usually associated with people with Buddhist monasteries, where people come to live in order to someday achieve enlightenment. At the same time, enlightenment itself is usually not taken seriously but is used to denote a certain unattainable ideal that one will have to strive for a lifetime.

Probably, touching upon this topic, I may seem strange to some but still, take a chance. Enlightenment is an absolutely real and quite strong change in the work of the human psyche that can occur as a result of the practice of meditation. I know because it happened to me. It happens suddenly, at one point. In Buddhist texts, one can find descriptions of several stages of enlightenment. Each of these steps leads to a radical increase in the basic level of awareness.

Achieving enlightenment is no easy task. But it is not impossible. According to Daniel Ingram, whose book gave me an understanding of the technical side of meditation, it is no more difficult than graduating from a university. And for this, it is not necessary to go to live in a monastery. If you meditate an hour a day and receive personal recommendations from an experienced teacher, I think it can take from several months to several years without interruption from your usual life. If you are interested, try to find such a teacher.

Meditation has a hugely positive effect on my life. I believe that the further you go, the more you will understand what I mean. Good luck!

Chapter 7 Clearing Out Your Energy Fields - Work with Crystals

Cleansing Gemstones and Crystal

An important tool when working with kundalini energy with chakra energy is crystals. The stone or crystal you intend to work with must be cleaned. The purer energy he possesses, the more powerful he is. Crystals should be cleaned immediately after purchase. A refined, ready-to-work crystal is filled with positive energy and is cold to the touch. The crystal that needs to be cleaned is hot, heavy, unpleasant to the touch. There are several ways to effectively clean the crystals and gemstones.

Sea salt

Sea salt is a traditional cleaner; it dissipates all illnesses and negative energy, serves as a physical and mental disinfectant. Sea salt is especially recommended for the initial cleansing of the stone and when the stone is full of negative energy. Salt can be dissolved in water or used in dry form. To prepare the salt solution, take a tablespoon of sea salt in a glass of cold water. Do not use plastic or metal utensils. Put the stone in the solution and leave it in it. When using dry salt, place it in a glass dish and bury the crystal in the salt. For complete purification, it is recommended to hold the crystal in salt for a day or two. When cleaning the necklace, it is better to use dry sea salt. If you live near a pond, it is better to use water from it.

Moonlight

Moonlight is another traditional gem cleaner. Bring the crystal to the moonlight (choose the time of the full or new moon). If possible, hang a necklace or place crystals on a tree, exposing the surface to the moonlight. It is not recommended to expose crystals to sunlight: many stones in the sun lose their color and may even break.

Herbs

Immerse the crystal in a cup filled with dried cleansing herbs. Good plants for the purification ritual: rose petals, sage, myrtle, frankincense, sandalwood. This is a very effective way to cleanse.

Earth

Crystals can also be buried in the ground. This procedure is especially useful when deep cleansing is required. Prepare a small, the size of your crystal, recess in the ground, put a stone there, and cover it with soil above. Notice the place.

Consecration of the crystal - Using your mind to heal

After you have selected and purified the crystal, you need to perform the ritual of its consecration. The purpose of this "programming" of the crystal is to concentrate its power and protect it from negative energy. A crystal or stone that is properly sanctified becomes much more powerful and useful as a tool. Take the crystal in your hand and feel its energy. If the stone was recently cleaned, the energy would be stronger and even more attractive. When you experience this energy, calmly ask for a higher power to bind the stone to the corresponding deity. Stones, in a certain sense, are living beings, and the deity of stone gives it energy and vitality. Once you feel that your request has been granted, consider how you intend to use this stone. If a stone accepts your intention, its energy increases. Otherwise, you will feel that the stone is not being charged with the right amount of energy. So, suppose you felt the stone was full of energy; now your crystal is blessed. You can now associate it with any deity. If you intend to work with the chakras, link the stone to the deity of the corresponding chakra.

Stone laying

The technique of using crystals and gems when working with the body is called overlay. This is a powerful method of getting rid of negative energy, cleansing and balancing the chakras, normalizing the emotional matrix, and directing the flow of light into all bodies. The cleaned, consecrated stone turns into a receiver and at the same time, into a transmitter of the good vibrations of space. He releases stagnant life force, directs it to the chakras, and also heals. Stones can be used both independently and in combination with laying on of hands (reiki technique). Stones are placed in places of physical correspondence of the chakras (note that chakras are not physical objects and we are only talking about their conjugation with parts of the physical body!), Starting from the legs and moving to the head. Use gems in colors that match the colors of the chakras. Stones can be of any shape.

Lie down. Place two light crystals above your head and below your feet (this ritual is easier to carry out together, with an assistant). In the right and left hands also take a crystal. Now start slowly placing the necessary stones in the areas connected with the chakras. If you suddenly felt uncomfortable when placing a stone, then this stone is not suitable for you; choose another.

When all the stones that you were going to use are placed, begin meditation on the deity of the selected chakra (or several chakras). Begin with the first chakra,

Muladhara, moving up. Visualize the deity, its strength and energy, feel its goodness. Visualize a bright color coming from a stone. Continue this visualization until you feel the need to move to the next chakra.

Lithotherapy: balancing your chakras with stones

To promote the balancing of our chakras, several methods exist, all having their own effects and influences on them. Once you have opened your chakras, it's time to rebalance them. One of the most effective methods is that of lithotherapy. So how does lithotherapy work, and what are its effects on your chakras?

What is lithotherapy?

Our body is in constant energy fluctuation, without stop, throughout our life. This fluctuation varies in intensity according to the events we live in everyday life, such as:

- Stress
- Joys and sorrows
- Cravings
- Fears
- Love
- Social and environmental interactions.

Usually, when all goes well, the energies circulate properly, and our mind keeps only the essence of our experiences (joy) to stabilize the balance of the chakras. This joy is recovered from one of the daily events. Only, when these are too intense, the chakra system can be disrupted and crash.

It is precisely to manage these fluctuations that the mineral stones can come to your aid. They are concretely the most effective to treat these dysfunctions, mainly emotional, and eliminate almost instantaneously most of the blockage.

To understand correctly, stones are always active on the same frequencies (unlike humans), which allows them to generate more good energy waves. What is called lithotherapy is the energy connection of the stones directly to the human, to balance his own energies, and to feel the benefits quickly. The virtues of crystals have been recognized for millennia because they were already present in ancient energy healing rituals.

How to Choose a Stone to Balance Your Chakras?

As noted, to choose the stone that will help to properly balance a chakra, it is very important that you have a good knowledge of yourself, your personal feelings, and especially your chakras. A simple trick to help you choose the right stone is simply to appeal to your curiosity. This is a great way to discover, as your experience with lithotherapy, the crystals that are most effective for you.

You do not need to learn them by heart: you just have to remember a few, the main preferences. For the rest, do not hesitate to check books dedicated mainly to and that talk about the subject, which will be much more detailed. Your learning must always be benevolent, never against heart.

Finally, your intuition can be an incredible engine to determine the stone you need. Generally, by instinct, you will always choose a stone that corresponds to you in the present moment, very often to harmonize the energies too present, or on the contrary, to help those who are under- effective.

Your body will always have the answer, listen to it!

What Stones Can We Associate With Your Chakras?

It would be too tedious to list all the stones and their many energy capabilities. Here is a summary of the main crystals and the different chakras associated with them.

1. The root chakra readily lends itself to easy balancing with Jasper, especially when combined with other minerals. Indeed, it relieves difficult digestion, gastric reflux, and constipation. Its beneficial actions have a very powerful impact on healing, but it also

significantly strengthens the tissues and the immune system. Directly connected to the root chakra it helps to harmonize it.

2. To balance the sacred chakra, try an orange stone such as Carnelian, Amber, Orange Calcite, or Bronzite. The benefits of Carnelian are mainly related to the adrenal glands and the management of stress.

3. To open your solar plexus chakra with a crystal, simply use Citrine. It is very effective: the vibrations of the stone directly affect the body, counterbalancing energy variations. Its field of action is vast because it also has an impact on the intestinal flora, the kidneys, and the pancreas. The solar plexus also likes Yellow Jade or Sulfur.

4. The balance of the heart chakra can be maintained using Malachite. This one allows detoxification of the body and promotes the energies of self- healing. Likewise, Aventurine, Emerald, or Green Tourmaline also have an important role in the well-being of the heart chakra.

5. To develop the communication of your throat chakra, use rather light blue stones such as Angelite, Blue Agate, Aquamarine. On the other hand, if you want to unlock the energies of your throat chakra prefer blue-

green and turquoise-blue minerals such as Amazonite or Turquoise.

6. If you are looking for the opening of your Third Eye chakra, the stones par excellence will undoubtedly be Cyclops Agate and Black Obsidian. To maintain intuition, letting go and concentration, choose Préhnite, Azurite, Cyanite, Blue Sapphire.

7. Finally, to heal your crown chakra, Amethyst and Lapis lazuli are recommended. Indeed, they clean your blood and play the role of an antiseptic for your body.

They are also full of good energies to evolve to a higher spiritual level and improve the clarity of your mind.

Once again, there is no secret: you just have to document to discover each stone one by one and learn more about their benefits.

A practical exercise in the use of stones

As calmly as possible, lie down with your arms around your body and empty your mind gradually. If you wish, you can light incense or a candle near you. Then, gently take the stone or stones you want to use during your treatment, and place them on the site of the chakra dedicated to it. Breathe deeply and quietly; it's not a race!

Now, disconnect dark and dark thoughts that disturb your relaxation. Focus on the stones themselves. You are likely to feel a sensation of warmth: this is quite normal; it is only the energy of stones that circulates.

Congratulations, you have successfully completed your first session of energy treatment with the help of lithotherapy!

Chapter 8 Demystifying Paranormal Activities - You Can Do It!

Astral Travel: How to "Get Out" of the Body

According to many esoteric teachings, in addition to our beloved, so-called dense body, there is also a subtle, astral body. It is a kind of soul that can travel freely in time and space. But this space is

special - astral. Non-physical, unearthly, light, and etheric. Material laws do not work in it, so astral travels are endless. You can find yourself in your past or future, visit the thoughts of a loved one, or even visit other planets. There is a working technique for entering the astral plane.

True, no one guarantees you that your astral body will leave the physical immediately, someone needs to train hard for a long time and hard, and someone flies out from a half kick. In order to disconnect from the physical body, it is necessary to become "easier" in the literal sense of the word. A short preparatory diet will help to "get off the ground" rather - drink plenty of water to start the cleansing mechanisms in the body. Do not overeat, increase the number of fruits and vegetables in the diet, limit or completely exclude meat: it is very grounding, but we do not need this.

Before you fall asleep or immediately after waking up, try the following: try to feel the shape of your astral body (this is not difficult, it exactly repeats your physical one) and move your toes, for example, without straining your muscles. This will be the first step towards the separation of the astral body since it is in such a dis-synchronism (the physical body is calm, and you make the astral move) that the separation of two bodies arises. When the practice of "moving the astral limbs" has already gone far enough, you can try to get out of the body, with a little effort pushing the astral out of the outlines of the physical body.

Do not worry and do not build grandiose plans - from high expectations; you often cannot get to the astral plane, no matter how clean the execution technique is. Along with the "astral movements," try to imagine what you are going to connect with and where you intend to go: your astral journey should have a clear goal, its direction.

When you feel incredible lightness and unusualness, you will see something that you have not seen before; you can safely say that you have been to the astral plane. Do not forget, by the way, to correctly return to the body - for this, just your firm intention to end the journey is enough, and remember - for any unpleasant sensations, the practice should be stopped immediately. Still, the astral is a delicate matter. Meditation helps.

Psychic Awareness

If we understand the psyche broadly, like the entire space of our inner world, then consciousness is then understood in the broadest sense - as the highest form of the psyche, namely: all those mental processes (internal information processes) in which a person can be aware of. Consciousness, in the broadest sense, is a process of orientation in the outside world and self-management, in which a person can give an account.

However, both the psyche and consciousness are often understood more narrowly, and then, if we use the metaphor of the searchlight, the searchlight of the psyche is directed outward and illuminates the outside world. The searchlight of consciousness is directed inward and illuminates the inner world: we get the opportunity to give an account of what is happening to us and in our souls.

Speaking of consciousness, it is important to distinguish between consciousness as a process and consciousness as a result.

Consciousness as a process is energy (power), which illuminates the inner world of a person and makes the management of mental processes explicit and controlled - the energy that carries light, power, and control.

Conscious - illuminated by the light of consciousness. A conscious hand movement is a hand movement that we track in detail, not an impulsive, but a controlled movement. A conscious objection is not one that accidentally flashed, unnoticed, but the one we looked at, somehow appreciated and which, as an objection, was allowed.

The unconscious is what happens in a person or with a person naturally, unconsciously: without conscious control and not requiring additional conscious effort.

Consciousness, as a result, is a person's inner world, but not closed, but open to external influences. Consciousness is an area of the psychic (inner world) available for internal vision, understanding, and control. The subconscious is a less accessible area. The unconscious is an inaccessible area.

All the functions of our consciousness at the present level of development are the result of evolution and conscious self-development.

In the early stages of his evolution, a man was far from being as intellectually and emotionally developed as it is today. His memory was not so full of information, and the ability to manage desires was not so trained.

True, in some other psychic properties - the sharpness of perception, certain types of attention that respond to physical danger, the strength of emotions, rage, which is responsible for survival, the ancient man perhaps surpassed his modern urban descendant in something.

But it should be recognized: in general, the psyche and consciousness have gone a long way in evolutionary development.

Again, meditation helps achieve this stage much faster.

Enlightening Compassion Through Your Heart Chakra

To unlock the energies present in our Heart Chakra, it is possible to use different methods and tools such as stones, essential oils, and Yoga posture. But in my opinion, it is essential to add meditation work, specific energy treatments, and reflection exercises.

It is important to know your dominant sensory channels to know how to rebalance your chakras in the simplest way.

The main sensory channels are:

The sight: the visual people will have facilities to visualize the colors during the meditations and energetic care.

Touch: kinesthetic people can use some stones, essential oils, Bach flowers.

Hearing: Hearing-inclined people will be able to align their chakra by listening to guided meditations, singing mantras, with the sound of the Tibetan bowl as well.

Conclusion

Hear reader, you and I have come to the finals of a very big deal, but I think you already realized that, by and large, this is not the final at all. Moreover, this is the beginning. I am sure that all the

best in your life is just beginning because now you are the owner of a great treasure: you have done everything to open your third eye, that is, activate your intuition!

It is very important not to fight her, to listen to her prompts, not to act in defiance. My intuition tells me that we will meet again and again. So, see you soon! I am always with you and for you!

Chakra Meditation

21 Days Guided Meditation to Awaken your Spiritual Power, Reduce Stress & Anxiety and Improve Awareness of Psychic Abilities with Reiki Healing Exercises

By

New Mindfulness Lab

CPSIA information can be obtained
at www.ICGtesting.com
Printed in the USA
LVHW020754270422
717291LV00014B/539

9 781803 036144